ekphrastics
&
eccentricities

ekphrastics
&
eccentricities

poems
by m. ann reed

© 2023 M. Ann Reed. All rights reserved.
This material may not be reproduced in any form, published,
reprinted, recorded, performed, broadcast,
rewritten or redistributed without
the explicit permission of M. Ann Reed.
All such actions are strictly prohibited by law.

Cover art by Chen Shuailang
Author design by Shay Culligan

ISBN: 978-1-63980-400-9

Kelsay Books
502 South 1040 East, A-119
American Fork, Utah 84003
Kelsaybooks.com

Acknowledgements

Warm thanks to the editors of the following publications who have believed in and made homes for these poems, some of which have appeared in slightly different versions with different titles.

AZURE Journal of Lazuli Literary Arts Group: "Bearing the Incomplete Sentence of a World Gone New," "Monet Meets Me at the Minneapolis Art Institute," "At the Mad Hatter-March Hare Art Gallery"
Burningword Literary Journal: "Sighting Polaris"
Cirque: "Abecedarian Song to Water"
Copperfield Review: "Painting Sunflowers"
Eastern Iowa Review: "Dandelions' Dream with Ray Bradbury"
Kallisto Gaia's OCITILLO Literary Arts Journal: "In November, the Horses Return," "It Could Have Happened Otherwise"
Oregon Poetry Association Contest, 2021 (Honorable Mention): "In Kiev, in March"
Pause for Paws online literary journal, Hong Kong: "Fire's Crackling Words," "To Begin Again—She Beholds Me"
Poetry Box, Poeming Pigeon: "Reintegrating with Earth's Divine Body, She Asks," "Planting Cosmos"
Proverse Hong Kong's Mingled Voices Anthologies: "Enough!" "Harvesting Lunar New Year Seeds"
Psychological Perspectives: "Anima et Animus"
Wild Woman Rising—historic online Literary Arts Journal: "Breaking the Alabaster Jar"

Contents

Monet Meets Me at the Minneapolis Art Institute	11
The Sea	13
Laugharne, 1989	15
Bearing the Incomplete Sentence	
of a World Gone New,	17
Telephone Telepathy*	19
Reintegrating with Earth's Divine Body,	
She Asks—	21
When Lost, Sighting Polaris—	24
It could have happened otherwise	25
Call Me Perdita	27
At the Mad Hatter-March Hare Art Gallery	28
Kindly Cautioned and Knowing	29
My Father's Celtic Cross	33
Who'd Have Dreamed	34
Reintegrating	36
Planting Cosmos	38
Breaking the Alabaster Jar Going Green	41
Dandelions Dream Ray Bradbury*	45
Enough! I Lacked Nothing	46
Harvesting Lunar New Year Seeds	48
In November	49
In Kiev, in March	51
Anima et Animus	52
Painting Sunflowers	56
Abecedarian Song to Water	57
Fire's Crackling Words	60
To Begin Again	62

About *ekphrastics & eccentricities*

These poems concern the fullest moment when art blooms with the artist and its resonance remains in time's timelessness. These poems also concern the fullest moment when life blooms among living beings before changing and evolving into further, fresher blooming, as shown by the *I-Ching's* twenty-four seasons of darkness learning to balance with light, with heaven and earth, until in each season, "they come together in the fullness of each chiaroscuro proportion" before they begin a new chiaroscuro or fulfillment to come. As such, these poems aim to honor particular artists and particular, even eccentric life moments, both meant to be shared.

m. ann reed

Monet Meets Me at the Minneapolis Art Institute

Spring-eluent,
    ineluctable genesis erasing
        winter burials: flights of stairs,

three-story buildings,
    sculpted ice,
        our burned bone marrow.

You enchant us with green Eros and pink Equipoise,
    charm us out to join earth's electric pulses
        and purposive lavender rain.

Yet Monet's *Rocks at Belle-Ile** disarm me most.
    Am I walking Monet's Breton Beach, negotiating
        that whirlpool rearranging the scene?

Is Monet's the only sun receiving sea-light?
    Who says the sea suffers into color no light of her own?
        A great grandmother cradling

me into her each splashing
    light-act of primary red, yellow and blue delving
        into precarious purple struggling

to be green, she reigns
    in her paisley light and shadow shawl;
        I flow into and out of mud feeling people stare

while Belle-rock refuges me . . .
    Someone behind me whispers,
        My soul is in this one.

Care(fully) I turn . . .
    There is no one . . . or is some One
        still everywhere changing

right here everything
    where no one's footsteps leave
        where some One remains to complete a rainbow?**

The Sea

The sea opens—
    a viridian heart drenching
        the shore in tears

then closes
    hugging longer the coastline's wrinkled
        touch

always drumming
    in waves
        always echolocating

the birth wail,
    the croon, the dance,
        the blow

and nuzzle of whales
    seeming to fly
        under the moon.

Bound as bodies
    to wild whales,
        we, too, move

and breathe
    and have our being
        in waves—

So where else would we find
    Dylan Thomas
        named *born*

from a wave of the sea
      to which he and Laugharne
          are beholden—

Dylan still composing in time's presence
      of the past his wavy lines of cynganedd*
          his native Cymraeg poetics?

Laugharne, 1989

Laugharne, laughing Laugharne,
      a lark caught in your throat,
nature dreaming through hard, hungry screams
      of gulls—

Laugharne, *hyvrid** Laugharne, a suppliant
      upon the beach,
a voice scattering light
      through dark waves—

dream naturing over rocks
      (always the 'll' through the teeth)
trickling up and out
      until river *Aberaeron** speaks.

Laugharne, who has known, still knows
      vicious minutes' hours,
the Dove haunts away a shaped and sharpened tongue,
      divests death of magical Laugharne.

Laugharne, burning on Dylan's lips,
      his soul a sandpiper scoping the beach—
a hand outstretched between dry bones
      (ground to yellow dust) and fertile mountains—

Laugharne, where we discover
      more sandpipers and suppliants
winding down now, *sea-shaken in salmon sun*
      with Dylan, with whom we run, we run—

Laugharne, where his song is a burning crested act
      kissed into emerald,
Rhiannon riding spring, moonless, slow—
      a breath on breath of indigo.

Laugharne, green *Cymraeg* cheating time,
       where the English demon lurks
in a country bus buzzing sixty
       'round hairpin turns.

Laugharne, where history is memory
       a schoolroom of *Welsh Nots****
The Mabinogion on wooden spoons carved
       by Hywer Davies of *The Strand*,

memory of a time everyone sang
       a song *Cymraeg*
then memory of Welsh known again
       as the foreigners' tongue

Mother English vying
       with Mother Cymraeg
while children cry
       from a circle chalked upon the floor,

For if we could we'd fly away,
       fly away
For if we could,
       we'd fly

Bearing the Incomplete Sentence
   of a World Gone New,

                               I ask how tender
can we bear to be—hear Laura's brother advise her
to *blow out her candles, for the world is lit by fire.**

Laura fascinates classmates with in-depth understanding:
"DiCamillo could have called her novel, *The Elephant's Magician,* because the elephant is always making magic, even when she's imprisoned. She expresses all the heartbreak and homesickness that displaced people feel—why she unites all who have lost parents' love, home, brothers, sisters, friends—why she draws out Peter's compassion—why she moves and speaks in Adele's dreams—why the magician can't let go of her perfectly magical being—why she is magnificent!

Laura's teacher humiliates her—announces, "Only quick and easy responses will gain top reading group admission." Posted are groups for all to read. Laura's name appears in the lower-than-she-deserves group. The top reading group protests, while Laura withdraws into her invisible carapace—that small turtle's cave of infinite inner freedom.

Laura notices the world's love affair with speed, emptying words, emptying rivers, emptying the earth of meaning. She notices the compulsive-aggressive cutting down of trees in her neighborhood (former home to evergreen nurseries and berry farms) all to make way for mansions. She realizes the atmosphere filling with quick and careless acts, and she determines not to give "quick and easy" answers merely to earn achievement badges—determines that achievements now mean bondages.

Laura blows out one birthday candle, sending flame's fiery spirit into the universe, and her voice blooms nightingale nocturnes; she blows another, and her eyes, lapis lazuli buntings, flutter in their nests. She blows two more, and wind floats her long brown hair shedding cherry blossoms into the starry, starry night. She blows three into light waves and particles roiling and rolling through midnight's blue silk cape sending out to dance all the animals from her rescue habitat. She blows, and roots descend—spiral from her feet joining the deep latticework of trees. She blows and feels the branches of sorrow weaving a new kind of joy. She blows and realizes why she has never felt so complete.

Telephone Telepathy*

Mary begins with a long, loose cursive 'p'
looping into a perfect Chinese cursive
character pausing to gather momentum
to change direction—to swirl into a bird's nest—
or circular web of lifelines as her telephone
telepathy begins—her friend speaking while she probes,
pencil on paper, the collective unconscious, her listening
hand drafting new understanding, creating intricate webs
within webs she will later ponder. For now,

she is listener—why her friends phone her.
Her brief responses show them she understands
as web after web fills up kitchen walls coded
by alchemical stages—*nigredo* for grief,
albedo for pure-hearted clarity,
citrinitas for finding new relationships,
rubedo for realizing integrity—
each evolving from different, but paired
golden proportional heartbeats breaking through
shadowed cobwebs to learn more than what might
have been trusted.

She trusts only her former musician's hand
and studies the new kaleidoscopic wisdom
until one day, the faint character on the page
whispered 'crisis-opportunity'—her best friend
had died from fifty prescribed, but undigested
pills. Shock necessitated time to pause,
turn the brush and begin a new direction,
but her hand read only her circling web of tears
as if a nest could contain her sorrow—
an incessant circling, reading the future
of broken lifelines as western medicine
would indeed change direction, empowering
big pharma and carcinogens poisoning earth—

Her circling becomes shadow after shadow,
a smoke screen for corporate profiteering
circling into the characters, *there's no going back*—

The future cloud of smoke she would not live
to witness—the genocide of the poor, the wildfire deaths
of old-growth trees leaving bereft young deciduous
branches *where late the sweet birds sang* now surrounded
by more smoke screens leaving whirling dervish counter
clockwise turns—oh, if only to turn back the time—
when networks between trees and humans kept in touch
from the underground world-wide web of trees—
teaching her hand growing more telepathy
because her unconscious knew more from its dark hug
than all consciousness become too small for us.

Reintegrating with Earth's Divine Body, She Asks—

what if you slept

and what if you awoke

to find yourself in the lap of night
    no moonlight   no streetlight   no candlelight

only a trinity of stars etched
    into the wounded deep shoulder
          wings of the mother

infinite   intense   light
    and what if she spoke to you
        you are the flower in my heart—
what if

to walk   to remember   how she had fed them—
hummingbirds purple finch sparrows northern
jonquils   dark-eyed junco harbingers of snow—
reminders among bare deciduous
branches, brown-curled bat-faced maple leaves lost
in sunlit morning of her once insatiable
longing for nature's mending art.
                      As she had fed
winter birds, they had fed her beauty and joy—
swept her soul clear—a perfect snow crystal.

Forest paths diverge: Old Main, Maple Fir.
Obie's Bridge . . . Wild Trillium marks logging-day
traces—abandoned cedar logs, decomposing,
entropic, feeding emerald moss and vigorous
ferns. Beneath growing cedars, toppled giant
maple limbs form dinosaur heads that pierce the air.

All had strained for light.
                        She had struggled, too,
in a dark time when Roethke finds *the eye*
begins to see—see rightly *only through*
the heart as Antoine de Saint-Exupery knows.

How many times have I seen her rightly
The mystery, not to be solved, but beheld.

After Stuttgart's Kristallnacht, she had witnessed
American citizens shoot German
Americans in the streets, witnessed them defame
Jewish synagogues, witnessed US Army
consignments: Conscientious Objectors
to labor camps, Japanese Americans
to concentration camps. Her German-Jewish
tongues, now demonized, failed her. She never
told this cautionary tale.
                        Had she forgotten
herself to become the lily pad anchored
within earth's watery navel—glad to fold her
hands, fine-tuned petals, into a peaceful pink cup—
accepted completely by warm afternoon sun?

So least her survivor's guilt remembering,
had she been so found? So blessed?

Tryon Creek bubbles up—courses through holly
and ivy land. A giant Norway Pine shakes
and draws me into enormous green arms
hiding birds singing evening's *joie de vivre*.
Wild peace, simple grace, natural rhythms die
to live anew; all inhabit this place
of nativities where ferns overflow
birch arches, marry autumn harvesting
and spring planting, both meeting in one time.

So why wouldn't I find, in this very place,
my mother who had always forgotten herself
in the green world filled with life's treasures
and enraptured birds to sing of them?

When Lost, Sighting Polaris—

that star-shine surpassing luminous sun's reason—my father found love and home. Polaris, sighting my father, set him to "making a home in a restless world,"* what would be his life-long labor of love. An architect under St. Patrick's wing, he joined the Irish Mayo doctors to transform hospitals into homes, redolent Rumi gardens and hospitality's arts.

Imagine being a young teen from Korea awaiting your sixth open-heart surgery in green garden's affectionate arms and returning this touch by touching red velvet Austen Rose petals while beholding "Earth's Children," the sculpture of hands and feet held around the globe and knowing that your two best friends in Seoul are holding your hands and feet. Or imagine being a widow confined yet buoyed by lazuli blue-bright sky erasing four walls to set sail with Chagall's dream of floating up, up, up into the cosmos of your wedding day with your lost, now found beloved—pausing on Beethoven's island of trembling Spring's Sonata Number Five and forgetting completely the tatters of your torn life. Or imagine the sculpted Rodin-like Asclepius whose arms surrender to uplifting you above desires and loathings to behold true cosmic north—home—homeostasis—hospitality—frontline of health, liberty, happiness, all besting the sapphire-hot joy of distant Icarus (once reliant upon Daedalus-wax and feather wings) now dancing joy's frenzy, not to forget how fragile we all are, but to remember our strength—our wise and medicinal innocence and our calling to make of our hearts a home to have and to hold, to liberate and to love what shines through all the bodies that cannot last.

It could have happened otherwise

It was inevitable, Dad.
It could have happened otherwise, Dad.
But it didn't, Dad.

You were defending a gifted artist's career choice,
though his father, your friend, threatened to 'disown' him.
You were driving home, pleading your case with Mom,
while I was listening from the backseat, searching
the starry night's incubating possibilities,
finding my golden thread spinning a halo around
my star—the hot blue one—and, likening you
to Shakespeare extolling mercy as true justice
(surely favorable to the artist's aim, yours
and mine) I announced my career choice to be
        a Shakespeare dramaturge.

NO! you exploded, so opposite your Irish-English
reticence, as simultaneously you braked
between city blocks—then fast-forwarded,
tumbling backseat grocery bags to the floor.
"But you supported—" "It's not the same!" you defended,
accelerating home while Mom floored invisible brakes
below the front suicide seat, which often fail to work,

and like Shakespeare's Viola, *all of her father's sons
and all of the daughters, too,* I morphed into your son,
Icarus, expelled out the car window, to try self-forgetting
unfledged wings that could, yet wouldn't fly with beauty—

How blind I had been. Hadn't known your story—
how once you had been a *wandering bark*,
a *country boy, whose worth is unknown although his height
    be taken,*
sea-tossed by city-slicker high school boys and bullied
by an English teacher you had nicknamed *Miss Macbeth!*
Your graduation photo depicts a gargoyle's face
suspended to ward off evil from the heights of a cathedral.

What *had* we learned? Had we redeemed our former
inner blindness? Realizing how *the course of true love
never did run smooth?* You creating beautiful rooms
and Rumi gardens for convalescing patients?
Me, gardening Shakespeare's world restoring justice?

Call Me Perdita

grounded
        into the vibrant
        porous
        circulatory system
        of creation

pregnant
        many layered
        monolith
        Stonehenge
        elusive
        unlocking shadows

my heart of light
        a poised dolphin
        speaking Ogham
        one more son of David
        stripped down
        to a hieroglyph
        too marvelous for me

marbled, adamantine
        whirled *anamchara*
        cum Ireland
        your soul friend

I accept your
        rainbowed weight
        drawing us up
        into blue arms
        holding our firm
        freckled flight

At the Mad Hatter-March Hare Art Gallery

Well, . . . What is it?
What do you see?

A wounded lion.
   A wounded lion who seems . . .

Seems to have ingested a lamb.
   Ah, your imagination, of course.

Yes, regard the mourning eyes.
   The part-lion-part-lamb lines.

Yes, lion lines appear . . .
   Superimposed over lamb lines.

Ah! She painted the lamb first, then the lion.
   A lion washes over a lamb; a lamb bleeds through the lion.

The tender heart forms the fierce, the gentle forms the strong.
   The artist's self-portrait as a child!

Kindly Cautioned and Knowing

I would be all of my father's sons
      and all of his daughters, too

I wondered what it would feel like
      to be the favored first-born—
           from dream edges I see him drift

away from himself—disappear
      into a grey world
           into four-lane highways

paved city streets through
      revolving glass doors
           a man with a gun (either behind

or before him) leading his escape
      into steel and poured concrete
           up a ghostly elevator

with ground lightning signals
      into windowless rooms
           there to spend his narrowing days

sometimes nights
      sending bits   bites   mega-bites
           without ever communicating

the feelings of words
      and all because of a glittering dark desire
           to be noteworthy

what privileged first-borns need to be
      to become the apple of their fathers' egos
           to relinquish their call—their life's purpose

in this case the accomplished musician
        he could be . . . perhaps facing poverty
                but never failure

Next door, Ghiberti's replicated bronze doors
        open Mayo's hospitable wings to sun   rain
                patients   physicians   frescoes abounding.

In the vaulted heaven above, Athena rests
        and arrests us upon her splendid shield—
                the seeing place—

a lesson in civic mindfulness commences—
        the surgeon plies his benevolent scalpel
                while Isis gathers her dismembered son—

inspiration raises whimsy's cloud
        on the shoulder of Pegasus
                and the cloud beneath his hoof claps

for all Prodigals becoming eccentrics
        breaking open like crystal-lined geodes
                the green shades of their emerald dreams

and I realize how difficult it is
        to transform desire for another's
                esteem into desire for bliss—

realize how this first-born cannot embrace
        what is truly his
                until he finishes loathing his life

Part 2. So, what *is* it like
         to be the estranged
              evicted Prodigal?

                   Completing my dissertation devoted
                to Shakespeare's *bio-poetics*
            lightning flashes and thunder growls
        through wall-to-wall,
floor-to-ceiling-windows.

I overhear
   "But I don't want to be a dentist, Dad."
      His clear voice carries over the phone
               through the open apartment next door

                        More lightning leaps
                  to inspire thunders' bellows
             a deluge ensues filling the silence holding
the father's rage.
   "I want to be—I'm going to be a concert pianist!"
      More lightning speaks blessing
            more thundering kettle drums cover
                 the father's response . . .

                     Altercation continues.
"A Norwegian conservatory has already given me a place,
   Dad. Dr. Balk gave me a recommendation.
   My aunt gave me money."

Lightning, thunder, and rain applaud
the wise, "Bye for now, Dad.
Talk with you from Norway."

I congratulate him across the threshold.
David Whyte's *Sweet Darkness* comes to mind
whispering *whatever* (or whomever)
doesn't make you come alive
is too small for you.

My Father's Celtic Cross

Up and up they float under their timeless
umbrellas as fierce rain pummels sidewalks,
and rebounds, drop by drop, as if knocking
on heaven to re-enter the clouds. "So, there *are*
many Mary Poppins in the world," I remark,
still a child, still a "Dream-Walker," as my father
        calls me.

Then the magic ceases when I learn the many
Marys are Mayo patients from all over
the world, whom the rude wind eventually
deposits on sidewalks far from intended
destinations. Soon iron railings surround
Henry Plummer's skyscraper, and patients
        are forewarned to hang-tight.

Soon Rochester, once rebuilt after leveled
by a tornado, boasts higher winds than Chicago,
and during one windy day, the cross atop
Calvary Episcopal Church flies the coop.

So my father, blessed by St. Patrick, patron saint
of architects, and blessed by his *anam cara,*
St. Bridget, carves a wooden Celtic Cross—
all those wee doors to new visions and insights
as gifts to the living from the Dead.

Though lower than Plummer's belltower carillon,
the new cross atop the church belltower
presides over this divided church in
a divided city. Though my father had hoped
these folks might settle differences, he settles
for the cross to bless the space between them.

Who'd Have Dreamed

the hollow growing point of a plant-cell
could shape a Celtic Cross—the soul's wee doors
inviting us into the Other World, leaving
us speechless, transported to where wise and witty
folk receive keen insights, there invited
to ponder how we might serve the world's soul!

Who'd have dreamed we'd share this astonishing
vision with botanist, Dr. L. "Watson" Roberts
whose revolutionary staining process
clarifies the spirit of this plant shining
from his book cover, aligning with quantum
physics discoveries—mingling spirit
and matter—what another botanist,
Emily Dickinson had found—a vision
surely received by ancient Irish sculptors
who had carved in stone this epiphany or dream.

Who'd have dreamed we'd be fireside-chatting
with "Watson" New Year's Eve, snow falling on
every part of Idaho, as once falling on Ireland's
New Year's Eve recounted by James Joyce's
Dubliners, into which we find ourselves
transported to mingle with the *fin d' siècle*
guests, whose voices come alive from *The Dead.*

We join Gabriel and Greta, portrayed
by Angelica Huston, as they re-cross
the threshold where Irish hospitality reigns—
      or does it?

While Gabriel toasts touted hospitality
celebrating his aunts' faithfulness, we mourn
with Greta and the warm, always open Irish
kitchen locked one night against Michael Fury
and his love for her. We hear the stones he had thrown
at her window-frame, while waiting for her
under wintry rain in a nearby garden
to bid her goodbye before next day
he dies—We rise with him to wake Greta,
quicken her even more to his love—evoking
her to realize what she had betrayed,
what she had always valued most . . . and we fall
with the snow becoming *general over Ireland,*
a frozen mercy loosed on every part,
dropping delicate snow crystals, cooling
Greta's hot tears, each offering wee doors
into the Green World never to be touched
by death, always here and now as our hearts open
        to collective dreams.

We fly home over the luminously green hues
of Idaho's Palouse, marveling the many
lives in one cell and how many lives we have lived.

Reintegrating

with Farmer Strong's old Holly Farm

rain sings tonight, each
drop bears candle flame,
an unwound clock

      4 AM, dad is always
      always meeting Saint Bridget—
      bridge between
      heaven and earth

forget your high G
unshelving—breaking
your mother's fine china—
green and magenta
star-fire hum in each raindrop—

      who says we can't go
      home or can't return?
      the bridge is always
      there humming for us

humming for the pink rose
asleep on forest floor
cradled by green velvet
feet of Oregon Beech
each drop bringing to bear
a seed of Norway pine,
a seed of Blue Spruce

      the home in our hearts
      still welcomes us still
      evolving as two
      are halves of one

low creaks of birch bent
by wind awaken us
to sleepwalking moans
of overgrazing horses
and the hiss inexorable of rain

though we moan with the horses
as if birthing new foals,
our roots and branches
breathe tranquility

and we return
to the green world
where rain sings tonight.

we have said *yes*
to Bridget

        we live inside
        green velvet feet

Planting Cosmos

Even now
Cosmos remembers her first garden—

the flaming head of Andromeda
cascading over the navel, the rose of Pegasus—

remembers*
her seed-life—

golden-proportioned
cosmic heartbeats

remembers
her roots anchoring into heaven's rich earth

remembers
love's Venus-water

remembers
gregarious star-chat encouraging her blooming

remembers
radiant light

awakening
the sword of her stem

piercing the dark
with life's green light

remembers
oh, remembers

the green wing-power
of her leaves

the universe held
by her calyx

the epiphany—
Hana—blooming

a new nebula
realizing herself.

What of Martin Reese's
*The universe does not exist
until I observe it?*

What of Albert Einstein's
*I like to think there's a moon
even when I am not looking at it?*

What of John Bell's
*What if an always aware finger
   (maybe the finger of God)
points everywhere always
there and there and here and now again here?*

Cosmos incarnate feels
the proper touch

the hummingbird hungry
for her nectar

the bee bathing
in her fragrance,

collecting
her medicine

loves the One
aware of her

remembers
the whole web-of-life

her role
to emit beauty

wonders: *what is your role
in the web of life?*

Breaking the Alabaster Jar Going Green

for street dancers accompanied by the cowboy song
"It's been a long, hard ride home"

Unhelmeted electric-powered bikers, we swarm
    Nanjing streets, bike paths, sidewalks—swoop
        soundlessly behind pedestrians, graze

calves with our passing shoe leather, all of us relentless
    racers to work. Our mission? Forced
        to workplaces on time or lose our jobs (despite

unmanaged high-volume traffic) we freely choose
    to support clean air. Only *wei guo ren* need remember:
        pedestrians sharing this mission lack right of way.

Safe awhile inside the stationary shop, you view
    our frenzy of fast development storming by, destroying
        the lives of people whom it aims to serve,

you view the unfolding drama as Eros and
    Thanatos write it, as Chinese view it—
        the past always before them, a rewinding film.

Perhaps you count mounted Venuses whose broad-brimmed
    hats challenge the promised, never delivered
        safety, their colorful silk scarves floating

behind them where their futures wait in blind spots,
    where Isadora Duncan's death by hanging
        replays as you imagine one of our scarves catching

in a turning wheel. Chinese art once shaped
    to make beautiful the space around it,
        now holds no value, yet you must admit

we Venuses have not lost our power
    to touch and transport.
        Inside our world of bright Sumi inks,

marbling and mingling with dark traffic,
    you sense beauty, truth and compassion coalesce,
        instilling uncertainty, mystery, curiosity.

Nearly trampled underfoot by others *going green*
    to board Saturday's bus, you *wei guo ren* ask,
        Does only forging ahead matter?

Recovering, you notice
    how robotic we Nationals appear, remarked
        only for hard work and efficiency.

You observe our lost body-awareness,
    lost intrinsic self-worth (recognized only
        by the jade on a red string around our necks).

Forbidden expressed pain or compassion's anger,
    you, too, regard the ironic government goals,
        "Safety and Efficiency."

Standing under air pollution's charcoal haze,
    painting the sun hazardous silver, you regard
        our wounds—family and community bonds

disrupted through Mao's protected informing.
    You understand why people still believe
        lies will protect them.

You realize that when fast is the way,
    nothing new can be learned—realize how
        compromised broken hearts lose zest for life—

realize how lost vigor and mindfulness
    become ennui's mantra, Mei *ban fa*—
        Nothing to be done.*

Still, Guan Yin nurtures the vulnerable,
    her devotees still nurture crickets—
        praying mantis, grasshoppers, ladybugs—

still follow, like their ancestors, the Chinese
    World Clock based on the *I-Ching*
        to live in harmony with nature.

One walks toward you, green in afternoon sun,
    the cyan sky accenting her flushed glow
        bearing a wood pole across her shoulders

from which hang two baskets brimming white,
    black and gold feathered chickens.
        You read each bird's incommensurable

worth—how for them,
    she lavishes her devotion,
        each feather a divine poem, intricate,

inextricable from the smile rising
    from you blooming just for her—
        her courage, her beauty, her shine

as she walks, fascinating, transforming
    the space around her until you are transported
        to the world made sheer with happiness.

Surprised, she feels your admiration and awe
    and accepts—returns the smile that bonds you
        into one feather liberated

by an infinitely gentle, still good hand
    writing a new heaven
        and a new earth.*

Dandelions Dream Ray Bradbury*

*to salvage a sunbeam's architecture
with their lives*

That the *Dent-de-Lion* is *golden* means it is as precious as the metal—unsurpassingly rich in sunshine, water and green sugar, homemade. That the *Dent-de-Lion floods* the world means it is as prolific as Bradbury—brimming over with gratitude and creative productivity. That Dandelions *drip* off lawns into streets and *tap softly* at cellar windows means they long to make new acquaintance. That Dandelions *agitate* means they shake, shiver and dance in Dionysian frenzy—ecstatic to be alive and awake! That Dandelions *dazzle and glitter with molten sun* means the sun hugs them and kisses them until they shine and molt like beautiful feathers from a most genial bird. That Dandelions are a *pride of lions* means they are a family of strength and *noblesse oblige,* offering their roots for tea, their stems and leaves for sweet summer salad and their flowers for medicinal wine. That they *burn a hole in your retina,* when you stare too long, means they are the sun's sensitive children capable of giving us a black-hole-in-space experience lest we become too arrogant. That Dandelions are *summer on the tongue* means their language is ours for the savoring, for the remembering of all the memories and moments we hold dear.

Enough! I Lacked Nothing

I desired nothing, wrote Meister Eckhart

Just so we felt at Lake Harriet,
    where ancient Lindens make a niche for us
        low in the s-curve of their trunks along the shore.

We perch, joining fanned branches of almond-shaped leaves
    curling slowly (like honey from spindle-spoons
        lacing apricot tea) into Autumn's slow drama.

Watermelon sunset marries Nature's fire, under-paints
    oaks and lindens, tints their olive, lime, teal, brown,
        and Chinese red barks pink-gold light.

Across a flaming sky, gulls float clustered
    like white lily pads, their water-wings flashing
        silver cutting edges of sun.

Is this the day you be waitin' for? Sings
    my brother's Black-American voice.
        A geode breaks open in my heart.

Lake Harriet, like another geode breaking
    open, holds the liquid sun wrinkled with
        amethyst crystals. Waves break into white iris,

cause pebbles under water to roll, emitting
    sparks, catalyzing water to grow, an offering
        to life's spirit.

Now the sun, a tiny golden ball (like
    the one lost long ago by a French princess)
        disappears in a moment, drops to rise

on the other side of midnight. Intense chill
    covers the land. More gulls rise, their wind-chime tones
        wailing lost warmth. An empty rowboat drifts.

Behind it, the Guan Yin moon—a splendid ripe peach
    nears to test ebony boughs.
        Transparent to night's cobalt entrance, moon's

jellyfish fingers meet phosphorescing grass.
    Woodland birds crack seeds. Seeds snap open like
        wood-burning logs. Snaps echo yellow finch,

singing *Papaveracea*. Closer now,
    the full moon pours ambrosia. Night chiaroscuros
        her form astride a graceful s-curve of trunk.

She is you; She is me
    lacking nothing, desiring nothing
        if for only this moment—

Harvesting Lunar New Year Seeds

on Mid-Autumn Moon Festival, we hear Chang'e
read,* exhaling her moon-imprisonment, her bones
bent beneath life's ten thousand grief's, her viola-voice
bidding good-bye to each spoken word, releasing
what is to recede: the sea, the past lives of stars,
her unchosen self. *Oh, give me myself!* she pleads,
and scatters ten thousand cinnamon sticks, from which
she reads her new fortune: *Morning is a garden,
a pear tree, a teacher beneath, reading to a child.*

She finds and sits with the child, Hime under
a pear tree, props a book on their laps, until both
are lost in *Wen Lin*—a forest of characters**—
this time Narnia's winter's forest, and wonder:
*Are pages, turning right to left, bringing us
into the past? Bringing us into white
witchery's world of frozen tyranny?*

*Or are we reading blindly backward into future's
unknowns?* Winged pages die into Oneness,
each flight-wave a resurgence of life—the butterfly
way to overcome tyranny's deception—revealing
a child's Big Dream—a child whose tiny hands
trust that *living is a form of not being sure,
not knowing what, next or how.*
                                        Now Chang'e knows
her old self who knew the story, but not its truth—
the moment you know, you begin to die a little.***
So, she releases knowing through her sad reading-aloud
voice; then breathes in each surprising silence—
each leap after leap in the dark— With each leap,
her new life wakes—she puts the lid on Yang's fire—
loving the moment when book covers meet and kiss.****

In November

    the horses return,
        night-watchers, gentle grazers,

holy presences
    of winter fur and eyes
        of dark water's light.

They return
    to share comfort and joy—
        the comfort of animal husbandry,

the tender care
    of daily watering,
        feeding, cleaning, brushing,

bedding-down,
    sheltering,
        veterinary hands,

and the joy of return,
    the white mare rolling,
        rolling her Dionysian downhill roll.

Neither north winds
    nor cold rains chill
        the steady flow of warmth,

the fire in their breaths.
    Noses nuzzle and kiss
        hearth and home,

kiss their feast
    moveable as flying feet
        kiss the old Holly Farm,

making sacred
    their pasture,
        their table spread

beneath conifers
    in the wilderness
        of their hearts.

In Kiev, in March

nature becomes white swans soaring under ice-pearl skies. Below, Byzantium's shards of gold shimmer with sun-setting pastels over deeply packed snow sprouting gold and green onion domes and Matryoshka-dressed women caroling honey-flamed cordials bringing goosebumps under gently falling snow. How silently these swans glide, watching over us and all who hibernate and dream warmly beneath frost lines. I am carrying thirty-two red-orange tulips, one for each participant in the first ever Women's History celebration. When I trip, fall on hard ice knocking-out my breath, if not my knees, releasing tulips into a perfect sunrise-sunset over milk-glass ice, I feel strong arms grip me from behind, astonish me upright with one shared inhale of a Heimlich-like hold, then quickly release me. I spot my angel stiletto exuberantly over wind-slickening ice, turning, waving to acknowledge my thanks, refusing the offered tulip while disappearing inside her home. Yet she is the one standing for all who had made women's history. She is the one who had, by transmission, initiated me into the women of Baba Yaga's wild instinct, the women who hold the tiny seed-woman's creativity beating golden measures of their hearts—

Anima et Animus

Alexander Agafonov paints and sculpts Ukraine's soul*

Part 1

You enter your life to bring to life the Mystery-Miracle Play
you dream, shape and
re-shape

You cross borders on unfledged wings, balancing with gravity
on stilts, feeling the world atilt with quantum-carnival
leaps

You explore painting's capacity to evoke sublime spirit and
sculpting's capacity to evoke Pan's ridiculous reclining,
balancing and fluting on the back of a wild running
boar—

     all this fettered-unfettered play with balance
because you had learned
to fall—

     first from an apple tree, landing at Hanna, the
healer's feet—that so-called witch whose candle in her
forest-cottage window promised unbidden
temenos

where your carnival dreams thrived in Pan's otherworldly
time to unfurl flying from your hand   an angel
                                         balancing

        on her invisible trapeze while
holding her candle to infuse day's light with a glowing
promise to deliver sky's
heaven.

You return her winged-waves with your brush-waves,
unburdening Kiev's spirit from protected informing, feral
dog packs, and
Chernobyl.

Your silent music shifts, too, releasing Sophia Mary, the
civil disobedient of her time, balancing feminine spirit
(undarkened by shadow) rising from new inner
light.

Her eyes touched by the *Mona Lisa's*, her smile a wisp of
Shakespeare's *Titania,* know *the path of true love never
did run smooth—*
                as from her accepted lily drops Kiev's
New Byzantium.

Part 2

Tender green sprouts begin to overwhelm the disarray—
rubble, burnt-blackened wood, discarded newspapers, ashes,
dust—
      while onion domes shine and bloom from sunlight's
wands

        from which your golden thread weaves a robe of
many vibrant colors welcoming back the lost communion
into your carnival of saints, all betrayed by protected
surveillance:

One, a brother whose sister had informed against him; one,
a mother, whose daughter had informed against her; and one,
a true knight who (masticated by a fierce wild Doberman)
had hugged miracles between
teeth.

Does the betrayed brother return, disguised in Harlequin's
patched suit shimmering from forest magic's candle
through transformation's
window?

Does the broken-hearted mother return, a new Madonna,
learning beauty's circumference
                            by balancing mandolin
with butterfly atop her
head?

Her gaze rounding to behold the child born of Gabriel's accepted message? Whose lily-shaped hand entrusts a messenger pigeon with his advice, *the enemy needs your Love*

Does your true knight morph into Pan? Protector of wild and feral animals, now fluting spell-unbinding music—
come away
i'm alive   come away
come away
do not take walking
for granted!

Followed by new lovers, *Anima et Animus,* who step out on-point to dance their
pas de deux?

You, too, take nothing for granted as you exhale back the halos** of your people joining the couple, bearing the new communion of fruit, flowers and
wine

from which your alchemy whirls vibrant oranges, ambers, honey-golds, greens, blue-burning Paschal flame until you shine

Painting Sunflowers

an ekphrastic of Dorothy Beryl Austin's oil painting

*would you like to see
my Spanish Sunflowers*
she asks full of sorrow
and hope

>under noon's
>Spanish sun
>three rise
>above the others
>
>brush strokes emit
>ragged
>withering
>petals—
>melting
>amber
>and brown
>oil
>
>one head drops
>intensifying
>gentleness
>
>aquamarine sky
>breathes
>liberty

>>Parkinson's neither shakes nor drools
>>through her when she paints
>>her hand steady as
>>a surgeon's, this time
>>not pruning, but liberating
>>the wings and petals
>>of a life complete

Abecedarian Song to Water

Agile mother of flora and fauna from Azaleas to African gazelles—now also partly acidic,

bitter from toxic additives on your palate, your various tongues acerbic, you do not become cynical, but clearly

candid, mirroring humankind's addictions, beliefs and inherited hubris, overestimating our progress— seldom

devoted to your way, your gentle underlying strength, your nurture of open-minded curiosity and benevolence, your capacious-hearted reading of earth's

electromagnetic sound and light-wave conversations— holding no bias, reading without judgment what all the living and the dead need to say—the cries of rocks, the reports of sand, the blue heron's hunger for love, fish and justice—restorative justice if we let the clear deep water of her eyes impress our gaze—forming

Faraday waves from attending Bach, Beethoven, Beatles, Be Bop, Rap, all shaking you upright to sing your reverence, lament, despondence, dark night of soul, revelation, alacrity, stand-up comedy, rapture, joy, all to transform metal singing bowls— and us.

Gregarious gorgeous gracefully nimble communication network—you are the tumbling, shivering, shaking streams of unconscious and conscious imagination from which Pegasus sprang to inspire magic's mystery, from which the *I-Ching's* dynamic chiaroscuros create the actual and possible tensions of new harmonies by which nature evolves.

Unassuming lighthouse of hospitality: Are you quantum physicist, John Bell's all-seeing eye, reflecting light waves pointing here and there and there, keeping an unrelenting vigil lest the universe disappear?

International Intelligence Agency, you hold more books than libraries. Judiciously meeting, reading, understanding multitudes of light and sound waves—even those of mitochondria and chlorophyll—you welcome cosmic immensity. Does your memory keep expanding? Do you share memory with elephants, who sometimes wish they could forget?

Kinesthetic cloud-sculptor, shapeshifter, are you the father of Raven, the trickster?

Lighthouse witness, welcoming and warning, your good counsel lifts us above mere senses. Are you

medium and message? Bearer of synchronicity's miracle? That shared longing of the universe to bond with earth?

Numinous, inspiring, you astonish and disarm us. Purr with cats at 50 hertz to mend broken bones and hearts.

Ouvre ton Coeur of music, to which dogs keenly listen, you are tuned to the muses and music of spheres to complete us until our lives come round right. No one's

predator, though forced by winds beyond your *métier,* you are always here to assuage, calm, succor into reciprocal balances.

Quixotic altruist, you are ninety percent of us as we swim our birth canals, endowing our eccentricities.

Robotic? Never!

Supple voice of sibilants and susurrus, you lull us into deep reveries—lucid dreaming, thereby

tipping our scales with No-Wheres Now-Heres* companioning our evolutions. You

urge us to revise our lives,

value our ground lightning-bestowed blessings

wending us around obstacles.

Xanthic sun's partner of photosynthesis, you make life's green sugar.

Yearning for equity, your language hones our lively paths. So please,

zoom us into our hollow growing points to learn care for you, not because of your overwhelming generous bounty, but because of who you are!

Fire's Crackling Words

    sputter into burned-out wood embers.
        Reverie's juxtapositions speak:

while the Chambered Nautilus Madonna holds
    a candle shimmering to light
        the Whirlpool Galaxy,

Dao Cat upstages:
    I do not know
        what it is about you—

you curl up
    in the red wool scarf
        by dying fire

bury your nose
    in your chest's
        black and white fur.

Ashes glow,
    wind stirs,
        your purr begins at 50 hertz,

mending broken bones
    as you stretch lengthwise
        on the Turkish rug

your paws kneading intricate patterns,
    opening—
        opening all your chakras,

each infused with love's firelight
    that births
        galaxies.

Rumi's voice emerges:
    What hurts you
        blesses you.

The darkness within another,
    unable to see the light,
        becomes another guiding candle.

To Begin Again

The world lives by beauty in excess of need.
                    —Wendell Berry

She beholds me—jet Black Lab bearing forehead
        wrinkles in time.

Bewildered, am I? I lift one eyelid
        sit for my portrait,

then rest my head on my blind Love's knee—feel
        Love's reading hands

assure me all is well. Bus rides can be tough.
        We sit up front—

she across from us, asking, "Have you read
        William Stafford's poems?"

My Love nods, "Yes, I've read some."
        "Have you read *waking*

to a new world brushed by a dog's deep love?"
        "No."

"Would you care to hear it?"
        We accept.

"Near your face a breath, your dog:
        'It's day'. . .

those dark eyes, receiver wells'* remind us
        to listen"—

62

we are responsible for Love's life.
    The poem doesn't end,

"It's day." Only the bus briefly stops.
    The world,

love-brushed, returns whole and new.
    I guide my Love

through our familiar-made-strange neighborhood—
    sense his keen reading

hand on my harness while we wonder why—
    how could we be

so blessed—so bewitched—so bewildered?

Notes

Monet Meets Me at the Minneapolis Art Institute
*An ekphrastic of Monet's Le Rocher du Lion painted in 1886 off the isolated Breton peninsula of Quiberon.
**Echoes from E. E. Cummings' poem, "Spring is a Perhaps a Hand."

The Sea
*A particular pattern of consonants and vowels difficult to transfer from Welsh into English.

Laugharne, 1989
*Welsh for lovely.
**Welsh for at the mouth of the Aeron River.
***1980s English forbade grammar schoolteachers to allow spoken Welsh and to post Welsh Not! signs.

Bearing the Incomplete Sentence of a World Gone New
*From Tennessee Williams' *The Glass Menagerie.*
A partial Ekphrastic of Vincent van Gogh's *Starry Night.*

Telephone Telepathy
*Ekphrastic of Joshua Eric Williams' "Still Cold History's Remaining Pages" found on *Rattle Literary Journal* website.

Sighting Polaris When Lost
**Reference to Scott Russell Sanders book, *Staying put in a restless world.*

At the Mad Hatter-March Hare Art Gallery
An ekphrastic of Dorothy Beryl Austin's watercolor and ink.

Planting Cosmos
The repetitions of remembers . . . shape a pastiche of an extract from Mary Oliver's long poem, "The Leaf and the Cloud."

Breaking the Alabaster Jar Going Green
*Samuel Beckett had satirized this refrain in *Waiting for Godot*.
**Reference to Revelations 21:1 and the I-Ching revealing how heaven and earth come together in the fullness of each evolving moment.

Dandelions Dream Ray Bradbury
*Italicized word choices are from Bradbury's novel *Dandelion Wine*.

Harvesting Lunar New Year Seeds
The Chinese Chang'e drank the elixir of immortality and was flown to live in solitude on the Moon. Here, she reads to the Japanese child, Hime, who also flew to the moon to escape forced marriage.
**Chinese Wen Lin refers to both a forest of characters or ideograms and a forest of literary personae. Reading is a matter of realizing meaningful complexity and many meta-worlds as the past flows before one, the future behind one.
***Echoes Agnes de Mille's advice to her dancers.
****The whole Chinese Mid-Autumn myth and ritual represent the separation between yin and yang energies needed for regeneration, the separation called "putting the lid on yang."

Animus et Anima
*With permission of the family.
**Reference to Marin Sorescu's *Prayer* translated by Gabriele Dragnea.

Abecedarian Song to Water
*Robert Romanyshyn's terms for meaningful displacement that elucidates the dream world.

To Begin Again:
*Content within single quotation marks are from William Stafford's poem, "Coming Back," in *A Scripture of Leaves*.

About the Author

M. Ann Reed offers the Bio-poetic Organic Unity Study of Literature in support of the Deep Ecology Movement for global and local academic students, some of whom publish. Awarded a doctorate in Theater Arts/Performance Studies, her continued education includes Jungian Psychology Studies. Her published literary essays are cited or remarked in journals of medicine, literature, and psychology. A Chinese calligrapher and brush-painter, her work has been exhibited in Oregon, New Mexico, and the Shenzhen Fine Arts Museum in China. University Press of America first published her book, *Strange Kindness*, co-authored with Mabel S. Chu Tow. When teaching overseas, she partnered with Paulann Petersen and Friends of William Stafford to offer William Stafford Birthday celebrations in Malaysia, Ukraine and Bosnia-Herzegovina. Various literary arts journals are home to her poems: *Antithesis, Azure, Burningword, Black Mountain Press, Eastern Iowa Review, Parabola, Proverse, Hong Kong, Psychological Perspectives* and *The Poeming Pigeon*. Finishing Line Press published her chapbook, *making oxygen, remaining inside this pure hollow note*.

About the Artist

Based in Nanjing, China, Chen Shuailang is a Chinese Rice Paper artist, sculptor, and space designer, holding an MA from Tsinghua University and a BA from Nanjing Normal University. She is a member of the Jiangsu Sculptor Association, an artist of the Youth Painter Academy of Nanjing Calligraphy and Painting Academy, and a cultural talent of Nanjing Bingyi Studio. Her creative works have participated in many exhibitions as follows: Jiangsu Modern Art Museum, Jinling Art Museum in Nanjing, Chinese Story Platform, Hehe Road Platform, Chinese National Academy of Arts in Beijing, Art Museum of Guangxi Normal University Press in Guilin, and Still Point Arts Gallery in USA. Her works and articles have been published in *Contemporary Handcraft* and *Chamber of Commerce Newsletter* in China, *Still Point Arts Quarterly* and *Psychological Perspective* in the USA, etc. Her *Rain Flower Stone series,* published by Shanti Arts, received their award of Uniqueness of Concept and Originality. She can be found @Chen Shuailang on Instagram.

Made in United States
Troutdale, OR
10/09/2023